ANOTHER LAND

Glimpses of Life in Prose and Poetry

Elizabeth

Elizabeth Fleet
Illustrated by Sandra Donohue

*Belated Happy
90th birthday
Mom xo Catherine*

 FriesenPress

Suite 300 - 990 Fort St
Victoria, BC, V8V 3K2
Canada

www.friesenpress.com

ISBN
978-1-5255-3917-6 (Hardcover)
978-1-5255-3918-3 (Paperback)
978-1-5255-3919-0 (eBook)

1. *BIOGRAPHY & AUTOBIOGRAPHY, PERSONAL MEMOIRS*
2. *POETRY*
3. *POETRY, CANADIAN*

Distributed to the trade by The Ingram Book Company

A copy of the card made for the Author by her co-workers
at the time of her departure for Canada in 1966.

For my family in Canada
and in England.

Table of Contents

Introduction 2

The World Around Us 5

My Arrival in Canada 6

From my Window 9

The Mystery of Life... 10

A Simple Request.. 11

Up the Down Staircase! 12

Creation 15

On Watch at Victoria Harbour★................................ 17

Ode to a Welshman★... 18

One Step at a Time.. 19

"My Home and Native Land"..................................... 20

Travelling★... 23

From a Hotel Window★ 24

"Are Grandma and Grandad Aliens?" 26

Early Morning by the Lake★ 28

A New Beginning 29

Waiting by the Lake★ 31

Take Time 32

A Message Shared 33

Windows of the Soul 35

Lost Glasses!... 37

From Laurel Point.. 39

A Silent Birth★ 40

Time Out.. 41

Evening Encounter... 42

The Touch of Love★ 43

Behind the Boardroom Door 45

A Walk by the River 48

Metamorphosis★.. 49

A Friend.. 50

Crossing the Columbia River.. 51

Network... 54

Alvin 55

Wednesday at Nine! 56

Overlooking Oak Bay... 58

Separation★... 59

Fifteen Minutes of Fame! 60

Change★.. 63

Destiny 65

Seasonal Paralysis★ 66

Winter Then and Now 67

Tribute and Celebration.. 69

Happiness 70

A Christmas Tradition 71

Perhaps... 73

A Dog's Life.. 75

Rock★.. 76

River of Life 77

Quiet Miracles.. 78

Wondering 79

O Canada!.. 80

Changing Seasons 82

A Gentle Message 83

Old Glory 85

Hiromi and Friends 88

Silence... 89

In Appreciation★... 90

Our "Best Friends" 92

The Grapevine 95

On Leaving Embetsu★ 96

Shining Forever 97

A Favourite Escape Trail.. 99

Always With Us 101

First Robin★ 102

The Fox Cardigan 103

Recollections 105

Last Day 106

A Summer Evening in Victoria 108

A Birthday Ode!★ 111

"Nothing Ventured, Nothing Gained!" 113

And Sometimes...Magic 116

Tapestry 117

Awakening 118

Closing the Circle 119

On Entering a New Year 123

Notes 126

Acknowledgements 129

About the Author 130

About the Illustrator 130

★An asterisk indicates that further information on this selection is available in the Notes.

List of Illustrations

Frontispiece: A copy of the card made for the Author by her co-workers at the time of her departure for Canada in 1966.

Never Lose the Wonder 4

Captain Cook on Watch 16

"Ships that Pass in the Night".. 22

A Winter Scene at Nancy Greene Lake 30

Such Intellectual Salmon!.. 36

Selkirk College 44

Crossing the Columbia River 52

Tika.. 64

Reincarnation! 74

Old Glory 84

The Bench.. 98

Hiking in Kokanee Park 110

The View across Eclipse Sound.. 120

The Mystery of the Future….. 123

…Will Complete the Grand Design................................. 125

Note: Each illustration is linked to a prose or poetry selection in the book, but it may not have the same title.

Introduction

Immigrants to Canada in the 21st century may come from almost any part of the world. Back in the 1960s it was very different: most of those who came to this country were white, and very often they were from the British Isles. At that time, teachers were greatly in demand. I had grown up in England, but had always wanted to travel, and in 1966 I applied for a teaching position in British Columbia. In August of that year, I was on my way to Montreal, going by sea as most people did in those days. I had accepted the offer of a teaching job in Prince Rupert and had booked to travel by train all the way across Canada.

Prince Rupert was a very welcoming place, but it was so different from where I had grown up. The language, in theory, was the same, but in practice it was very different, as I found out quickly when I started to teach. In addition, I had been hired as a social studies and physical education teacher, but I was quickly informed that, "All the social studies teachers teach a block of English." This meant that I would have to teach poetry!

I did not dislike poetry; in fact, I remembered as a young child making up various little verses and feeling quite jubilant. In school, however, none of my English teachers had an inspiring way of teaching poetry. I feared that I might be the same, but what happened that year surprised me. I did not fall into the trap of asking the students, who were in their early teens, to do the initial reading of a poem to themselves. I read aloud to them, and then we would discuss the content of the piece and different aspects of poetic language. I wanted them to enjoy poetry in the same way that one enjoys music, for its sound, and I was surprised how well the lessons went. I had always enjoyed writing and had written short prose pieces. It was at that time that I started to make up some poems of my own and discovered how much satisfaction there can be in finding exactly the right words to express one's meaning.

It was many years later, in discussing poetry with then Lieutenant Governor of British Columbia, Dr. David Lam, that he said to me that he thought of poetry "rising above other language in the same way that cream rises to the top of milk." To me, it was a beautiful analogy and kept me working away in any spare moments in family life. In due course, I shared some of my work in small gatherings and wrote various pieces for celebrations and other events. On several occasions, a prose piece or a poem was read on CBC Radio.

In recent years, I have wanted to gather some of my favourite writings together for family, friends, and others who might be interested. Much of the content of this book comes from my love of nature and the outdoors. Other pieces that I have included are more generally philosophical or family based. There are also a few samples of works written specifically for other people, and some which relate to my close ties to Selkirk College in the 1980s and 90s.

Occasionally, when reading a selection, it is helpful to know some background, and an explanation is given on the same page as the piece. On other occasions, when I wish the reader to develop his or her own ideas first, an explanation is given in the Notes section at the end of the book. Many of the poems or prose works are about common themes and experiences which require no background information. I foresee the book being used most often for random reading of a few selections, rather than being read straight through from beginning to end.

All of these pieces have been written during fifty years of a very happy marriage. Some are intensely personal, but often reflect common life experiences. Writing has always helped me to sort out my values and ideas, and many of my best poems come from times of questioning, whether in relationships, child rearing, religion, or some other realm.

People often sew, knit, or garden for satisfaction and for fun. My search for fulfilment and enjoyment has been in creating tapestries and designing flower beds with words!

Elizabeth Fleet
April 2018

The World Around Us

Treasure all creation.
Cherish it with the love of a parent,
But never lose the simple wonder of a child.

My Arrival in Canada

I was 23 years old in 1966 and had been working as a Map Research Officer for the Ministry of Defence in England. The other staff were very kind to me when they heard that I was heading to Canada. They presented me with a briefcase and a beautifully crafted card wishing me well. I had accepted a teaching position at Booth Memorial Junior Secondary School in Prince Rupert, British Columbia.

On August 18th, various family members and friends saw me off at Euston station in London, and I travelled by train to Liverpool to board the ocean liner *Empress of England*. My parents were working in Kenya at the time, and there was a telegram from them wishing me good fortune in my adventure. It was a time of excitement for me, but of apprehension too; I was leaving a country I loved and heading into the unknown. I watched with curiosity as other passengers on deck threw toilet rolls to their well-wishers on the dock. As the ship left, the toilet paper unravelled and eventually broke, emphasizing the separation that was taking place. It would take five days for us to reach Montreal. After a brief stay there, I would start another five-day journey from Montreal to Prince Rupert by train.

The passage across the Atlantic Ocean was an amazing experience. I found myself at a table with four other teachers and three nurses, all planning to work in Canada. Everything was wonderful until the fourth day, when news came that there might be a rail strike when we arrived. The next day we were lining up to seek travel advice. I never did find anyone else booked to go as far as Prince Rupert! I was advised to scrap the plan I had to stay in Montreal for three days, and to get on the first available train.

"That way you will be sure of getting to Winnipeg," I was told.

I knew that Winnipeg was only half way across Canada, but I had little money, and when we arrived in Montreal I had no choice but to do as advised. After a night and all the following day on the train, I did indeed reach Winnipeg, along with 25,000 others, all seeking alternate modes of transport! My only choice was to get on the Greyhound bus. I could take my suitcase, but my trunk, with any school materials, would have to wait until the strike was settled. I left Winnipeg on the only Greyhound bus that I have ever known to accommodate standing passengers.

A day and a half later, at six-thirty in the morning, I was dropped off at Cache Creek, in southern British Columbia. This was the junction at which I was to wait for the bus north to Prince George. There is very little at Cache Creek even now, but fifty years ago there was even less! I waited…and walked around…and waited, for nine hours in the August heat, until I finally boarded my next bus and travelled on for another seven hours or so. Prince George was very much a frontier town in the 1960s, and more than a little educational for a 23-year-old travelling on her own! I somehow survived the inexpensive hotel near the bus depot, and the next evening I caught the bus for the last leg of the journey west to Prince Rupert.

In those days, Highway 16 was paved only in short sections around the main towns. It was a gravel road experience for almost all of the 700 or so kilometres west from Prince George. At one point, somewhere near Hazelton, I awoke early in the morning and saw a black bear beside the road. I wanted to voice my excitement to the whole bus, "My first bear!" but all the other passengers were trying to sleep.

The last fifty or so kilometres, from Tyee to Prince Rupert, were the worst part of the entire journey. I had left Winnipeg on a Thursday evening and by then it was Monday. I had always had a tendency to become travel sick, and my own exhaustion and the twisting and turning of the road were simply too much for me. Somehow, I made it through without disgracing myself on the bus, but I have never been so relieved to reach a destination!

I was met by a representative of the School District and the young woman with whom I would be sharing an apartment, and within a short time I was feeling much happier about things. My trunk, with any school materials that I had packed, arrived six weeks later, at the end of the strike.

That first journey across Canada certainly made me wonder a little about my decision to travel. Teaching in a different country had its interesting times too, but Prince Rupert was a friendly, welcoming place, and I met my husband Terry there. This year, 2018, we celebrate our Golden Wedding Anniversary with a family reception and an adventurous safari in Kenya and Tanzania. It is with happiness and some awe that I look back more than fifty years to those early days and the challenges when I first arrived!

From my Window

Crisp and tingling February air –

The bright sun glistens
On shrinking remnants of the winter's snow;
Hoar frost, clinging to each tiny twig
For a few short hours,
Transforms the trees and bushes
Into mysterious branching corals,
Stretching stiffly into a sea of blue.

Glistening frost,
A sparkling mantle,
Will subtly be withdrawn;
Brilliant in its splendour...
And then, in moments, gone.

The Mystery of Life

How can we mortals understand your plan?

We watch your hand unfurl the miracles of nature:
The beauty of the lily,
The matchless miracle of birth,
The majesty of mountains.

We see your spirit in the deeds of others:
A caring friend,
A generous gift,
The trusting ties of love.

And then, it seems, in cruel jest you strike:
A youngster crippled in an accident,
A dying mother with her mission incomplete,
A baby born with cruel deformities.

How can we understand your plan?

Take time to watch the ants,
Running with purpose in search of food.
They comprehend in their own terms the elements of life,
Yet have no concept of the gardener's great ideas.
And even animals,
Who may be closer than our human friends,
And understand hunger, fear and love,
Will never comprehend the thread of human life.

We see but dimly what your purpose is;
We cannot hope to understand...

We simply must accept.

A Simple Request

Do not judge me now…
Live a day first and see;
Tread in my footsteps,
Feel for me.
Walk a mile in my moccasins,
Let our paths be the same;
Know my joy and my anguish
Before you cast blame.

Up the Down Staircase!

Before I left England in 1966, I diligently looked up the city of Prince Rupert and found out all I could about it. I had accepted the offer of a teaching position there and planned to stay two years. After that I would either head on to Kenya, where my parents were living at the time, or return to England. I certainly did not think of my departure as "emigrating"!

The challenge of getting to Prince Rupert during the rail strike was over, and I had met the other English teacher with whom I would be sharing an apartment. In talking to her, I started to learn more about the issues the local school system faced. She mentioned that the turnover of teachers every year was about 50%. Most Canadian teachers only taught in outposts like "Rupert" until they could obtain a position in a less isolated location. Many of those who filled vacancies were from other countries, especially England and Australia. This was not a surprise to me, for on my voyage across the Atlantic the entire table at which I sat in the dining room had been made up of teachers and nurses on their way to jobs in Canada.

Prince Rupert itself had, and still has, an interesting diversity of nationalities. A high proportion of the population is First Nations, especially Tsimshian. As a fishing port, the city has also attracted immigrants from other fishing nations, particularly Norway and Japan. In perusing the phonebook, and later my class lists, I found that the majority of the names were challenging either to pronounce or to spell or both! Ironically, those names that were familiar, such as "Bolton", had a high chance of being First Nations people.

In due course I settled in and visited my new school, Booth Memorial Junior Secondary, which in those days accommodated students in Grades 8, 9, and 10. My homeroom would be Grade 8's. I looked at the classroom in which I would be teaching and immediately wondered whether I had done the right thing in being so adventurous. In the corner, just behind my desk, was an accumulation of plaster which had, presumably recently, fallen from the ceiling! My room was in the original multi-storey brick building, which dated from around 1920, and was adorned with several fire escapes on the outside. One of the first warnings that teachers were given was that the fire escapes must never be used for any purpose as they were likely to come away from the building!

I had just read the book *Up the Down Staircase*, which was all about a first-year teacher's experiences. In that old building we did indeed have an "up" and a "down" staircase, and it was also my first year of real teaching. That combination of circumstances made me more than a little apprehensive! When I was given my timetable, I found that I was to teach some English, and on questioning this, I was informed that all the social studies teachers taught English. Although I had always enjoyed writing, in England I would not have been considered qualified to teach English, having had no regular instruction in language or literature since I had passed my O-Level exam at sixteen. Did this mean that I would have to teach poetry…to thirteen-year-olds? Perhaps I should have applied to a school in England or headed straight to Kenya, where my mother assured me that I would have no difficulty in finding a prestigious teaching position!

One's first year of teaching is always hard. To attempt that first year in a foreign country was even harder. My three months' teaching practice in England had been in a small girls' grammar school in Somerset and seemed so irrelevant at a junior secondary school in Prince Rupert! My students would sometimes remind me that they could make more money on a fishing boat in the summer than I made in a year, which was true at that time. In the meantime, I was slaving away every night trying to keep one page ahead of my classes in such subjects as Canadian history, which had not received great attention in my own education!

Then, of course, there were the PE classes! My degree from Cambridge University was in geography, and when I took my teacher's qualifications at Bristol University, I had chosen physical education as my second subject. At school, I had been captain of the tennis team and the netball team; I had played field hockey in university and had passed the Royal Life Saving Society's Award of Merit… None of this helped me to teach volleyball or softball, both of which were completely unknown to me. Unfortunately, the English game of "rounders" did slightly resemble softball – just enough to cause trouble! I well remember the occasion, and ensuing embarrassment, when I asked who would like to be "fourth base" – there being four bases and a home plate in rounders!

Somehow, with the confidence that only young adults can muster, I did survive, despite using all the wrong terms and being teased about my accent! I can even say that I had time to enjoy my second year of teaching, though the old building was condemned that year and the whole school had to go on shift. I found that I actually enjoyed teaching poetry and even writing some poems myself. In due course I even became one of the volleyball coaches and accompanied the school teams on a trip to Alaska.

In retrospect, I think almost all the students were remarkably kind to me. They cannot have known how insecure I sometimes felt!

Creation

The artist, working silently beneath the sky,
Transcribes the scene with skillful motions of a brush.
Composers, on lifeless, five-lined paper,
Build up the beauty of harmonious sound.
The architect and sculptor dream shapes of beauty.
The writer, with diligence, selects, discards, rewrites,
Before a word is born.

All these create.
Yet, are not they, in all their skill,
Much humbler than the Great Creator?

Who formed the rugged beauty of the mountains,
And gave us sunset and the starlit heavens?
Who breathes the life into a newborn child?
Who first created man?

A greater artist:
One who, with patience far surpassing human powers,
Observes the universe;
Changes and perfects it as the years pass on.

And yet this Greater Spirit still allows
Created to attempt creation;
And now and then, a deep ethereal beauty is revealed —
The gift has been passed on to human hands.

On Watch at Victoria Harbour

The sun sets in radiant beauty,
The harbour a joy to behold.
Queen Victoria stands at her duty,
Watching her boats leave the fold.

And Captain George Vancouver,
From his pinnacle up in the sky,
Can see all the way
To the end of the bay,
And issue commands from on high.

Not far from his two companions,
With his back to this wondrous sight,
Stands Captain James Cook,
With a woebegone look,
Never seeing the sunset at night.

While others can gaze at such beauty,
Looking out at the ocean swell,
This bold pioneer
From an earlier year,
Who at sea conquered all,
Has his face to the wall.
He is destined to stand,
At his maker's command,
Staring straight at the Empress Hotel!

Ode to a Welshman

Did he come from Aberystwyth,
Or perhaps from Pontypool?
From Llandudno or from Snowdon,
Where the mountain winds blow cool?

Is he a man from Harlech?
Most famous are their men…
Or did he hail from Ebbu Vale
And desert it way back when?

Like any other Welshman,
His voice goes up and down
As he tells his rugby tales
With glee to everyone in town.

I can't recall his name now;
Was it Jones…that rings a bell;
Williams it might have been…or Hughes,
Or Thomas would do well.

We come on this St. David's Day
To present you here, forthwith,
This beauteous leek as token,
And with it – "Cymru Am Byth"!

Note: Composed for a Welsh friend, Deon Miskell.

One Step at a Time

Hour by hour,
Day by day,
We face life's trials on our way.

Week by week and
Year by year,
Such tiny steps our fortunes steer.

In years of joy,
We gain our strength
To cope with sadder times at length.

When life seems hard,
Its fruits unjust;
In times of deep despair, we must…

Hour by hour,
Day by day,
Take smaller steps to ease our way.

"My Home and Native Land"

Young people leave home and travel for many different reasons. There are those who seek adventure or opportunity, and those who simply seek temporary change and new experiences. In our world today, there are also many who seek refuge from war-torn countries or relief from famine and other desperate situations. There are the happy, optimistic travellers, and there are the struggling migrants whose lives have been devastated. All are, for one reason or another, leaving what they call "home". Some may intend to return at a later date; others know that they will not.

At what stage does one's adopted country become "home"? All new immigrants wrestle with this question, especially in the early years. The answer may be "never" for those who constantly crave what is missed from their native land and who live in hopes of returning. On the other hand, I, feeling intense loyalty to Britain in 1966, and having no intention of emigrating, now know that Canada is truly my "home".

I recall that when I first arrived in Prince Rupert, I constantly compared what I saw and experienced with the memories I had of England. Often, I found myself thinking that a certain item or practice was "better" in England, especially if I was feeling in a critical mood anyway. This tendency slowly mellowed, and I occasionally began to notice things that were different, but that I could allow myself to think of as "better" in Canada.

There were many British settlers, especially teachers and nurses, in Prince Rupert at the time. I became aware of a tendency for those who had come to Canada as a couple to give serious consideration to returning, while single people were often more open to permanent change. Inevitably for a couple, the decision to emigrate is harder; both families are left behind, and there is the possibility in the future of grandchildren growing up isolated from both sets of grandparents. Single people have more freedom – but in 1966 I had no intention of emigrating!

One's circumstances and emotions can change so quickly. At first, I was living in a basement suite with Joan, another young English teacher. In less than a year, a young Canadian, Terry, came to board with the family who lived upstairs. There were two other male boarders at the time and one female. All of us often enjoyed our spare time together as friends, and almost as a family, as none of us had relatives close at hand. One of those friendships grew into a romance, and in 1968, Terry and I were married. This was a total change of life plan; letting go of my previous convictions, I had decided to stay in Canada, and I was happy. My father even said to me at the time that, if he were my age, he might well make the same decision. That said, for many years I still spoke of England as "home".

When did things change for me? I can pinpoint one exact time when I realized that my loyalties were less settled. We were watching the final of the Commonwealth Games women's high jump competition in 1970. The two main contenders were from Canada and from England. I was forced to choose – and it surprised me a little to realize that I wanted the Canadian to win. These precise moments in one's life are few, but that was one of mine.

In 1975, I became a Canadian Citizen. I wanted to be able to vote in my adopted country and had developed a love and respect for all things Canadian. Fortunately, this did not require me to forego my British citizenship, and to this day I maintain my British passport. Does this in some way show a divided loyalty? Perhaps, but it is impossible for me to wipe away my family still resident in England, the first 23 years of my life, and my experiences and friends from university days in Cambridge. Those loyalties remain, but as an example of my Canadian allegiance, I now support fundraising efforts for Selkirk College in Castlegar, because I am sure that Cambridge University finds it easier to raise money!

I rarely, if ever, speak of Britain as "home" any more. I love my adopted country and feel accepted, yet Canadians nearly always rec-ognize my origins. My friends and relatives in England have become used to my mid-Atlantic accent and my changed choice of vocabulary, but they still make me feel so welcome – almost as if I had never left. I believe dual citizenship is a totally valid concept, but I have never encouraged our children to seek the British citizenship for which they can qualify through me. They were born in Canada; it alone is their country, unless they choose otherwise.

My "home"… emphatically yes! My "native land"… not in the literal sense, but enough to sing *O Canada* with enthusiasm!

Travelling

What ever happened to the lady at the airport;
The one whose mother had died the week before?
She poured out her grief to me,
As if confiding in a friend,
Until our flight was called.

And later, on the plane,
The lean and youthful volleyball enthusiast,
Suffering the taunts of his team-mates...
"Travel-sick," they said out loud;
Then whispered of the last night's escapades.

And where, now, could I find the excited family
Who waited in the restaurant
For their trans-Atlantic flight,
The two small boys pleading, repeatedly,
For, "Just another quarter for the games machine?"

What of the anxious couple who waited on standby?
Or the neighbour, who squinted to see just what it was I read...
Then looked the other way in case I smiled.

Where are they now,
Those ships that pass in the night?

From a Hotel Window

I watch in freedom from the fourteenth floor.

In early morning light,
Magnets draw the traffic to their poles.
With seeming purpose, people, like scurrying ants,
Direct themselves to reach their goals by the appointed hour,
And start another busy, tedious day.

Offices light up like fish bowls, stacked in rows;
Nameless automatons busy themselves
Around machines.
As an illusion of freedom,
A tennis court stands unused,
Perched incongruously atop an office tower.

At noon, as if in momentary hesitation,
Busy minions leave their desks
And grope towards freedom once again;
Only to be drawn back, as moths might be enticed
Towards a dazzling light,
Not always knowing what they are about,
Allured by forces stronger than themselves.

As daylight fades, the workers are disgorged
To struggle to their homes,
Be fed and rested,
Live a while…
Then face the unnatural pattern once again.

They are benevolently imprisoned
In the lifestyle of our world;
Programmed to accept this servitude.

What would they do if given freedom now?
Perhaps observe the incongruities
Which we in our supremacy have here created.

I watch the scurrying ants.

"Are Grandma and Grandad Aliens?"

It is good to recall some of the wonderful questions small children pose: "Why don't our heads go all the way round?" "Where does God live?" "When do numbers end?" When I was asked by our youngest what the word "alien" meant, I started by saying that it was someone from a different country – a foreigner. That was what precipitated the question about Grandma and Grandad… who lived in England!

Our children always knew that both sets of grandparents lived a long way away. This of course had impacts on them, and also on us. All three were born in the Skeena Valley of British Columbia, one in Prince Rupert and two in Terrace. I also lost another infant at birth in Terrace. My parents were in England, and Terry's parents, who still had two of their seven children at home, were two days' drive away in Kamloops. There was no question of relying on help from them. In difficult times, we had to count on friends or neighbours, but we did try to ensure that visits to our children's grandparents were sufficiently frequent to maintain a relationship. In the in-between times there were many reminders when we looked at photographs and spoke on the telephone.

In some ways, raising one's children without an older generation looking on can be "freeing". It can of course be helpful to have advice, which I sometimes had in letters or on the phone, but it is also good not to have the pressure to treat a new generation exactly as their elders were treated. My childhood in England was very stern and restricted in many ways, but circumstances and attitudes towards children have changed since the 1940s and 50s, and they continue to change. Nowadays many young parents seem to depend to a high degree on the grandparents for babysitting and "time off". This was not so common in the 1970s and 80s, and certainly not available for us.

Terry's parents tried to visit us once a year, but for several years their visits included two of his younger brothers, and once his grand-mother came also. Our children looked forward to those visits, but they were very short. "Nana" and "Granpy", though they lived in British Columbia, had to drive a long way to see us, and they had to spread their time amongst their seven offspring. My parents, on the other hand, lived in England and could not visit every year, but when they came, they were often with us for three weeks or a month – long enough to get to know their grandchildren and take part in some of their activities. They tried to come every three years, and we made trips to England as often as the "England Fund" would allow, usually about once every four years. Fortunately, none of us was hurt in our car accident in 1974, but it was sad to see all the England Fund sacrificed to replace the vehicle and a trip to see the grandparents delayed by a couple of years.

When we moved to Castlegar in 1980, our time with Terry's parents did increase somewhat as their circumstances changed and the last of their family left home. Jeremy stayed with them on one occasion, and Terry's mother was very good at organizing family reunions. On our visits to England, my parents always tried to have all three children for two or three days to allow us a break. In the 1980s, they settled into a routine of coming to stay with us every other year at Christmas time. They loved the different traditions, the snow, and the seasonal decorations.

By the time Terry's mother and my father passed on, in the late 1980s, all our children had lasting and happy memories of their time with grandparents. My mother continued to come for Christmas until she was 89 years old. Our friends and our children got to know her well, and Canada became an important part of her life. She was far from "alien"!

Early Morning by the Lake

Perhaps a way of praying –
Walking on my own;
Regaining God through nature,
Peacefully, alone.

Putting in perspective
Our superficial way;
In silence, thus,
My soul is touched
And strengthened for the day.

A New Beginning

Darkness surrounds us, curled in confinement;
The humble beginning of all human life.
Nestled in comfort, cocooned from all danger,
Loved and protected and free from all strife.

Why should we move to the next stage of being
When we can rest here in tranquillity curled?
To be born is to die from all that we value;
Why must we journey on into the world?

Existence brings change which we're destined to follow;
We move from the womb to new lives of our own.
We grow, and we cherish the friendships and beauty...
Then cling to life here, to the joys we have known.

Curled in the womb we could not see our future,
But found we were loved and had nothing to fear.
Our journey continues; death...just a horizon...
The limit of vision for us waiting here.

We entered this life not by choice but by destiny;
Loving hands cradled us here on this earth;
And we can be sure that beyond the horizon
This love will continue at our second "birth".

Waiting by the Lake

Snow falls gently, floating down;
Builds unwieldy loads on bending branches;
Partly fills tracks, leaving a ghostly hint
Of what was here just yesterday.

Skiers stride like stickmen through the snow;
They push their way through powder,
Breaking trail around the frozen lake.
The late ice-fisherman rubs his hands,
Then packs and heads for home.
Clear voices ring through cold, still air;
The distant drone of traffic speaks of a world
For once so far away.

In the rustic shelter by the lake the burning wood
Crackles a cheery welcome in the stove;
Snowy footprints lie un-melted on the floor;
The firewood in the corner keeps its coverlet of white.

Strange voices penetrate the silence
With loud, abrasive tone.
May they pass quickly,
And not desecrate this island of tranquillity.

Take Time

Take time to know the beauty of our world:
To watch the moon rise on a clear, fresh, summer night,
To see the dewdrops glisten on the grass,
And sense the cleansing ritual of a storm.

Take time to wonder at the miracles:
To see the fresh, green leaves burst forth in spring,
To smell the velvet fragrance of a rose,
And listen to the stillness all around.

Take time to hear the laughter of a child,
To walk with friends in sadness and in joy,
To give the comfort of a fond embrace;
To listen, to smile, to love.

Take time to ponder what our role on earth should be;
To value happiness and peace of mind;
To cherish the very gift of life itself,
And live as just one part of this our world.

A Message Shared

Do we recall the struggle endured at birth?

No.

But then we were too young to understand.

At other times our understanding fails us too;
We are too young again.
We question, feel pain, lose faith, dread parting...
Wonder why.

But some it seems have greater wisdom;
Endure with grace the trials of rebirth;
Shine as a beacon in the darkness of our doubt.

The memories you have scattered as our friend
Can be for us like seeds;
Which, nourished and protected,
In due time...

Bring forth their fruit
And give us reasons why.

Your twinkling smile,
The message in your eyes of humour, mischief, sympathy, or love;
Your quiet, gentle, laughter and your faith;
Joy and completeness built in family;
Gentleness, strength, and love amongst those held dear ...

These will be ours in memory;
The seeds are sown for us,
And we give thanks.

Note: Written in memory of Ab Dunn, a counsellor at Selkirk College. He died in 1994. His wife, Donna, is still our close friend.

Windows of the Soul

The windows of the soul
Convey their quiet messages.

We glimpse a little of what lies within:

A spark of happiness
In eyes that smile,
The open gaze of love and trust,
A twinkle of joviality,
A hint of fun.

But grief and sadness also play their role:

Perhaps a look of hatred and distrust,
Or desperate eyes that cry in fear and pain;
The empty gaze of those now left alone;
The eyes of hope and pleading...
And the stares of resignation and despair.

Silent messages pass through
The windows of the soul.

Lost Glasses!

This is one of the funniest Fleet episodes ever, and one which has been shared countless times, generating much amusement. It is almost too ridiculous to be true...but not quite!

It was the mid-1970s. We were living in Terrace at the time, and Terry was a keen fisherman; not necessarily a successful one, but keen nevertheless. Our children were small and not really into fishing yet. Occasionally they and I would accompany him, but at other times he simply went with a friend for some "escape" time.

On that particular day, Terry and his friend Mike set off to the Kalum River, a tributary of the Skeena. The salmon were running already, and the two fishermen had high hopes. Selecting the pool that has greatest potential can sometimes take quite a while. Is the current too fast? Are there too many snags? Are there other people around? After half an hour or so, Terry and Mike had settled on a place of great promise. It was a quiet pool at the side of the river with a large fallen tree stretched along the bank, offering a perfect vantage point.

With the selected lure in place, Mike walked along to the root-end of the fallen tree, which overhung the water, and there he made a few casts. This was a good spot and every now and then there would be the encouraging sound of a fish jumping somewhere within earshot. Things looked just perfect! Mike was just reeling in a cast when suddenly an angry hornet came up from under one of the tree roots. Wasps are one thing, but large hornets around the face are quite another. As the buzz came closer, and the threatening insect circled his head, Mike swept his hand across his face in an effort to deter the aggressor. At that point, somehow his hand connected with the side of his glasses, and sure enough, they were swept from his face and fell straight into the Kalum River. Considerably disadvantaged and distressed, Mike carefully came down from the log and contemplated whether there was any possibility of a salvage operation.

In the meantime, Terry, always a loyal friend and now having a far superior ability to visually assess the situation, climbed along the log to the exact point where Mike had been fishing, so that he could have a better look and possibly help in the salvage attempt. He was not there more than thirty seconds when the hornets, angry at being disturbed yet again, sent a further messenger up from their nest. And here is the part which is hard to believe! In rapid and determined motion, Terry brushed another rogue hornet away from his face, and in no time at all had completed exactly the same action as Mike. His glasses too went flying down into the river!

It was a deep pool. There was no possibility of retrieval, and two grown men came home from their fishing expedition earlier than expected. It was not unusual for them to return empty handed, but this time they had the added embarrassment of having both lost their glasses! We like to think that for the remainder of the season there were two very erudite-looking salmon swimming in the Kalum River!

From Laurel Point

The air outside is chill; the sky is dark;
The city lights around the Inner Harbour
Are mirrored in still waters there below.
Lighted floors of buildings
Merge in reflected splendour,
Resembling a line of candles
Dripping their streams of coloured light
Into a pool of darkness.

A time to ponder gentle memories,
Reflected and shimmering in the ocean of the past.

A lighted fishing vessel nudges its way to port,
Leaving a wash of glistening ripples
Playing in its wake.

A scene of quiet contentment…yet,
In anxious toil and turmoil, unaware,
The world will glibly pass such beauty by.

A Silent Birth

You struggled hard to reach the distant shore;
In darkness strained and kicked, but all in vain.
You longed for life, elusive, hard to gain,
And begged for freedom, groped towards its door.
We beckoned through the ocean's heedless roar,
And prayed for you to reach the yielding sand;
We watched and willed and waited, hand in hand…
Then, in a dreadful darkness, heard no more.

Your heart was still; your body lifeless lay;
You drifted to the shore, and there you slept.
Your strength was sapped before you reached us here;
Around you loved ones, unbelieving, wept.
A silent bond will hold you ever dear;
We loved you and remember to this day.

Time Out

That evening, for half an hour or more, I sat outside on the small balcony adjoining our bedroom. This was nothing unusual, except that it was almost ten o'clock and dark, and from the crispness of the air, I was sure that we would have our first frost.

I thought of writing outside, as I sometimes do, but I knew it would be much too cold. Instead, I simply grabbed an old checkered blanket from the closet, stepped outside, closed the sliding door, and curled myself into the lawn chair. Yes, a lawn chair, old and a little worn, but always there, throughout the year, ready for me whenever I needed it. I wrapped the blanket closely around me and sat in the darkness; alone, but not lonely.

The moon was almost full, proudly monopolizing the sky and dwarfing the faint outlines of the Big Dipper and other familiar shapes. The air was clear and crisp, and the moonlight so bright that the sky was not black; it was a hazy grey, and even tinged, it seemed, with a relic of blue. In contrast, the mountains across the river were black and foreboding, revealing only their silhouettes.

The moonlight shone down on eddies in the river far below: shimmering, alluring, deep, and mysterious. The moon itself seemed big and comforting; a benevolent presence, so far away, yet somehow seeming close.

The sky, the moon, the mountains, the river: these are the constants, and we the transients, who sometimes need to reconnect ourselves to nature and to eternity. In the stillness of the evening, somehow tensions were eased. The world seemed far away and unimportant. I breathed the crisp, cleansing air, shed my cares as if in a prolonged sigh, and felt a deep sense of peace.

Evening Encounter

Sometimes, it seems,
Our Great Creator smiles with mischief,
And purposefully plans "coincidence".

Each walked alone,
Until they met by chance;
Surprised each other,
Journeyed on together.

Was it by chance?
Or did a greater mind
Act playfully and smile?

The Touch of Love

Stay close;
Be with me at my journey's end,
And hold my hand as I pass from this world.

When I was born, hands held me first;
I learned to walk, clinging to those close by.
I loved and was loved, held close in tenderness;
I grieved, and friends enfolded me in their embrace.

Now, life is passing from me, hold me...still...
And let me know, once more, the touch of love;
In silence I can then move on with strength,
Seeing more clearly outstretched arms ahead.

Stay close,
And hold my hand...
Then gently pass me to the welcome of rebirth.

Behind the Boardroom Door

For almost twenty years, starting in the early 1980s, I was closely involved with several advanced education institutions in British Columbia. First, I was a board member for Selkirk College, then for the Open Learning Agency/Knowledge Network, and then for Royal Roads University. As time went on, I became more and more convinced that one of the essential qualifications for a board member is a well-developed sense of humour. Some of my experiences in the early days can perhaps provide a taste of the lighter side of serving on a board.

I remember the greeting I received from the President on my first visit to Selkirk College, immediately following my appointment:

"Mrs. **Sleet**. I'm so pleased to meet you!"

This made me feel more at ease. I had never served on a board before and had worried that I did not know enough about Selkirk College, but this built up my credit to make the odd mistake or two myself. In my first few months as a board member, every second word spoken seemed to be an acronym, and I began to wonder if I would ever learn the intricacies of the language. I listened intently, said relatively little, voted as my conscience dictated, and hoped for the best. Slowly things began to make sense.

When graduation season approached in Castlegar, each of the regional high schools requested the presence of a Selkirk College board member to present the Selkirk Award. It was a pleasant task and a chance for one's role to be recognized by the public. My early history in this regard was disastrous, though through no fault of my own!

On the first occasion, I made the necessary brief speech and felt that things were going reasonably well...until the chosen recipient came onto the platform and solemnly informed me that she did not qualify for the award, as she was not going to Selkirk College. I whispered to her that we would sort it all out later, whereupon she re-iterated quite loudly that she would not be attending Selkirk College! This is a moment of my board career that I remember very vividly!

The following year, although my fellow board members teased me about not being capable of presenting the award, I was sure that things would go better. Once again everything started well. I announced the winner of the award, and this time he was indeed due to attend Selkirk College. Little did I know, however, that my award winner was one of only two graduates, of well over a hundred, who had elected not to attend the ceremonies! For a second year running I returned home having failed to present my award.

As the years passed, my experience broadened, sometimes more quickly than I anticipated. On one occasion, the board chairperson was to make the official presentations at the Nursing Program graduation. I planned to attend, but simply as an observer. It was a cold day, but bright and pleasant, and I decided to don my old, very functional, snow boots and walk the short distance from home. I knew that I was not dressed for elegance, but then no one would be watching me; their eyes would be on the "important people." We all sat quietly for some considerable time. Eventually, one of the Nursing Faculty approached me and apologetically reported that they were all waiting for the board chairperson, but that he still had not arrived. Would I mind taking his place?! Complete with the healthy outdoors look and my snow boots, I strode valiantly to the front of the hall!

In 1988, my learning curve steepened considerably when I was elected board chair. I was enthusiastic, but did feel that others had more widespread experience. A month or so later, it was with some trepidation that I led a new board member orientation session. I was humbled right at the outset when one of the new members pointed out that the zipper in the back of my skirt was undone! Surely things could only improve after that!

What of board meetings? There were certainly those times when a slip of the tongue by one of the board or the administration could result in grins askance, expressions of surprise, or even outright laughter. Take the "Return to China", for example. When this topic was introduced at one particular board meeting, eyebrows rapidly rose, for just the previous week two board members and an administrator had come back from Japan! Questions ensued, but within a few moments the board was relieved to learn that the reference was to the purchase of permanent dishes for the cafeteria in lieu of styrofoam. There were definitely no plans for people to travel!

Occasionally there was confusion with names too. Captain Wood, who was a board member, was on one occasion introduced as Captain Cook, and a few months later George Westinghouse, a faculty member, was introduced to the board as George Washington. At least, in both cases, these name adjustments heightened, rather than lowered, the prestige of the individuals!

Behind the boardroom door at Selkirk College, or any of the other institutions with which I have been connected, there were no deep dark secrets – merely dedicated individuals, who worked away quite seriously, but sometimes needed to laugh at situations, and sometimes even needed to laugh at themselves!

A Walk by the River

Evening calm descends;
The heat of day is eased
And Earth breathes freely once again.

Along the river bank the crickets chirp;
Killdeer raise their plaintive cries
And run to guard their young.

Wild flowers, bordering the trail,
Have quickly overgrown and dried with heat,
Yet still lend summer fragrance to the air.
Differing shades of green
Mass on the nearby mountain slopes,
Beneath the clear, blue, cloudless sky.

Majestic winding river, far below,
Seeks its unseen goal with calm intent;
Ospreys soar with elegance
Around their nesting place.

As twilight subtly steals away the day,
All is at peace...and nature too seeks rest.

Metamorphosis

Within that hardened shell,
Slowly changing,
Waiting for nature to take its course,
A partly formed butterfly is enshrined.
Traces of beauty lie concealed;
The task is only partially complete;
Around these hints of elegance
Confusion still abounds.

Slowly dismantled, not yet reassembled;
No longer playful and open, the little girl we knew,
But private, abrupt, attacking the unknown...
Better left alone within her shell
Until these subtle changes are complete.

In time she will emerge with quiet grace,
A joy for those who watch, and wait, and care.

A Friend

A true friend is like the beauty of an evening sunset:
Perhaps not a necessity,
But one of the joys of life.

Crossing the Columbia River

The Columbia River rises near Invermere, in British Columbia. It flows adventurously north at first, then curls around the Selkirk Mountains and sweeps south through the Arrow Lakes. It passes Castlegar and Trail, flows into Washington State, entrenches itself in the Columbia Gorge, and finally flows into the Pacific Ocean at Astoria; an impressive journey of two thousand kilometres.

We live in Castlegar, on the west bank of the Columbia. This was the ancient home of First Nations peoples, including the Sinixt Indian Band, and it was part of the region explored and mapped by David Thompson in the early 1800s. Our house stands about two hundred feet above the water, and just north of the elegant Columbia River bridge on Highway 3. This has been our home since 1980, and the magnificence of nature feeds our souls daily. We remember particularly an occurrence in 1997.

That winter, the snow piled up to more than four feet, and the ground lay covered from early November to late March. It was very cold, and for several weeks the snow was hard enough to allow one to walk unhesitatingly on the frozen crust. One Sunday afternoon, a group of us hiked down the Selkirk College trail on the east bank of the Columbia. We walked along the shoreline, and on the opposite side, right beneath our house in fact, we saw three or four deer at the river's edge.

As we walked further, we suddenly spotted another deer, on our side, quite close to us and apparently startled by our sudden appearance. It pranced along the edge of the trees in an agitated manner, and then, to our horror, started to walk out into the frigid water. The Columbia and the Kootenay Rivers have their confluence at Castlegar. The newly born, greater Columbia is wide, deep, and turbulent. The thought of a deer trying to cross the river in near-freezing water was horrifying. We felt a sense of guilt, as if we had forced the animal into an action of panic, but of course we could do nothing.

Our eyes were riveted to this little body as its antlered head bobbed slowly along. Swimming at an oblique angle, with the current but just slightly across it, the deer calmly showed us his intention. It was about five minutes before he emerged on the far bank, just beneath our house. Perhaps he had not planned to join his friends at that time, but he knew exactly what he was doing.

The Columbia can be turbulent and angry at times, but mainly it is a source of great tranquillity, and we are privileged to watch its magnificence and witness the beauty which it nourishes. In almost forty years we have only on that one occasion seen an animal swim across the river. We watched with the awe that humans sometimes feel as they witness the miracles of nature.

Network

Network…
Build connections…

Spread,
Branch,
Extend,
And make your contacts.

Too much,
Too many,
Spread too thinly with too little time.

Then filter…
Screen…
Gauge value and assess.

Dispense with those who cannot help your climb;
Measure your time…
Yet always keep those gold card contacts;
Pathways to the top.

But…
When connections fail,
And when the superficial web gives way…

Where then are friends?

Alvin

The artist, standing at his easel,
Holds creativity within his soul,
Not just his hands.

A composer, deprived of hearing,
Can be surrounded by music
In a silent world,
And still pass the message on.

An athlete, in his prime,
Shows the inner strength which drives his limbs;
The will that cannot be defeated.

Our limbs, our senses, aid us in life's journey;
Tools which we can use
To express what lies within.

The beauty of a painting is born within the mind;
Music is an expression of the soul;
The true strength of an athlete is his inner self.

Even a simple hug…is from the heart.

Note: This poem was written for Alvin Law, a motivational speaker. Alvin was born without arms, and in the literal sense unable to hug. Metaphorically he hugged us all.

Wednesday at Nine!

Perhaps it is the small-town spirit! For many years, when we lived in Terrace, I was part of a walking group that met regularly and enjoyed exercise and social time. All of us were busy women with families, and we particularly relished the opportunity to be with other adults. Our family's move to Castlegar in 1980 was exciting in some ways but distressing in others; for one thing there would be no more Thursday Walking Group.

During that first summer after the move, I found myself talking to another mother while the two of us were watching swimming lessons. She seemed to have some of the same interests as I did, and I risked asking her if she would be interested in a walking group. We have never looked back! The Wednesday Walkers was formed that fall, and we were fortunate enough to add to our numbers one who was very familiar with the numerous trails in the Castlegar area and could also identify the different wild flowers. In the early days, our time was quite limited as some of us still had young children. I had to be back home by the end of the morning kindergarten class, so we did not walk for long, but it was wonderful to have an opportunity to meet new people and then finish with a quick coffee at one of the participants' homes.

When all our children were in school full-time, two things happened. Firstly, we were able to take longer, more ambitious walks, and secondly, some members chose to return to work, but there were always enough people to keep things going, and eventually everyone retired! Those who worked part-time tried to avoid working on Wednesdays, and none of us would make dentist or other appointments on a Wednesday unless it was absolutely essential!

The group has continued to thrive, sometimes almost too much when there were twelve of us, plus dogs! At one stage, we compiled a cookbook for a younger member who was getting married, and we have held Christmas parties and other get togethers at various times. Some people have moved away, but we are still in contact with them, and there have been ten, twenty, and thirty-year reunions. There will likely be another one in just a couple of years!

When the Wednesday Walkers was formed in 1980, we were in our thirties, but now we are in our sixties, seventies…and almost…! In our social time, we are no longer discussing the problems of young children, adolescents, or aging parents. It is more likely to be our own aging or the accomplishments of our grandchildren! What used to be a quick coffee time has morphed into an extended lunch, and at least once a month, we go out for our refreshments. Although the routines have changed a little, the principle is still the same; we all want to get some exercise and we all enjoy getting together. There has never once been an atmosphere of "gossiping", and in so many ways, we have given support to each other at our different times of need.

We walk in sun, rain, or snow, and have very rarely cancelled. The one thing we all try to do is to keep our Wednesday mornings free!

Overlooking Oak Bay

Time of tranquillity;
Brief respite from the turmoil of the day.
Dining at leisure,
Savouring an interlude
Free from the trivial urgencies of life.

The bay before us lies serene and calm:
The sea washes contentedly on barren rocks,
Revealing and concealing them with passing tides.
Low wooded islands cluster close to shore,
As tugboats seeking shelter from a storm.

The sunlight slowly yields to the dusk,
And, one by one, the tiny fishing boats,
Defying the ocean's warning jibes,
Push daringly to sea.

Life, pictured in slow motion…
Relaxing hours pass in quiet companionship,
Watching the day stretch slowly towards the night.

Separation

Cleanly cut,
And, in a moment, separated –

A new life in the world.

Yet from then on
The bond regenerates.
Two lives are joined again,
Through joy and trauma
Growing with each other.

Tempered by life's experiences,
The ties grow slowly stronger;
Separate lives,
Yet inextricably entwined,
Dependent on each other.

Then, quietly,
That separation reappears;
This time a slower, wrenching pain,
Tearing away the years which have passed by...

Yet, in its way, once more
The herald of new life.

Fifteen Minutes of Fame!

It was an experience that I shall never forget! I was the focus of everyone's attention, and the onlookers were not friends of the family or even people whom I knew.

The year was 1990. I had been staying in England with my mother, who had been widowed the year before. At eighty-four, she was facing the challenge of living alone amazingly well. We had had a wonderful three weeks together, and that morning we were waiting for my brother to arrive. He would take me to Heathrow to start the long return journey to Vancouver. After one night there, I would be heading back to my family in Castlegar.

I would not want to describe my mother as "fussing"; "caring infinitely" would be a better description.

"Won't you let me make you a sandwich? You might be **so** pleased to have something with you!"

We had already discussed this possibility. I had said, quite resolutely, that I would not need any food for the journey. Nevertheless, when the topic came up again, and I knew that my mother was already wondering how long it would be before she saw me again, it just was not worth the effort of protesting. Why not simply agree? After all, she would never know whether I ate it or not! A sandwich was never more lovingly prepared: cold roast beef and lettuce, carefully wrapped and accompanied by a few little home-made extras.

"There! Oh, I am glad you changed your mind!"

It was hard to give that last clutching hug and speak bravely about the next time my mother would travel to Canada, but we were well practised. The tears sometimes rolled, but mostly afterwards, when we were on our own. My brother arrived. I was swept up with military efficiency and in no time was on my way to Heathrow to board the flight to Vancouver. The visit had gone well, but I was looking forward to getting home.

Time passed quickly on the flight. There was no shortage of things to eat and drink, and I never once gave a thought to the sandwich in my flight bag. It was quite a luxury to travel without children, and I enjoyed it. Before long, I was filling out the customs forms, and then, an hour or so later, landing at Vancouver. Along with other weary passengers, I made my way to the luggage carousel and waited for the Boeing 747 to give up its load.

As I stood there, my eyes lit on a beautiful little beagle. I supposed it was travelling with someone, but I was drawn to the dog rather than to its owner. As it made its way closer, I thought I could read "Ministry of Agriculture" on the little green jacket it was wearing. "How interesting!" I thought. I had never seen a beagle on patrol in the luggage area before. I suspected it might be looking for drugs.

It is amazing how quickly the whole focus can change! I had been looking outward: watching other people, keeping an eye on the carousel for the last of my luggage, and admiring the beagle from afar. Quite suddenly, I was aware that everyone was looking at me! As if drawn to a dog lover, my canine friend had found its way over to me and had even sat down right next to my feet, between me and my flight bag. For a split second I felt specially privileged. Then the reality set in; when the beagle sits down, it has "found something"!

At a full six feet, I have always felt conspicuous in a crowd, but never as much as I did on that occasion! All eyes around the carousel were on me, and one could just imagine the conversations:

"Well – I'd never have thought it!"

"She doesn't look the type now, does she? But then...you never can tell!"

The dog's handler was quite pleasant and asked me if I had anything I wanted to "tell him about."

"No," I said, "I hardly brought anything back."

"Not carrying any plants or meat products that you haven't declared?"

"No...Oh...Oh dear! I think I know what it might be."

I swear I had not given my meat sandwich a thought from the minute I had put it in my hand luggage until that moment. As my fellow passengers watched, I took all the contents out of my flight bag and at the very bottom found the offending object!

The official was very kind, but needless to say I ended up in the slow line for customs clearance. Every one of my bags was thoroughly searched, but fortunately I did not have a connecting flight, and I was able to see the humour in the situation. My mother enjoyed relating the story to her friends afterwards, and of course in her eyes I was a celebrity!

Change

The chapter ends;
The story vibrant to the last, full, satisfying word,
But now the page must turn…

And all is blank,
As if the author pauses to perfect
What is to follow.

The past holds unplanned triumphs
In an unexpected role;
Struggles and fearfulness;
Challenge and success;
The joy of striving hard toward a goal.

The future, for now,
An echoing void.

In time the story will go on,
The emptiness will mellow;
The feeling of "alone" will disappear,
In chapters yet to come.

Destiny

Six tiny, helpless, newborn shapes they lie,
Exhausted from their journey to the world.
Protective, as these strangers come nearby,
Around the sleeping brood their mother curled.
They have no strength to stand or even cry,
And eyes so tightly closed, as if in sleep.
Their needs in her own way she'll satisfy,
Their instinct bids them near her warmth to keep.

Will this weak, wrinkled, handful now be changed
By food and loving care and nothing more?
How can this helpless form be re-arranged
Into a loyal and loving Labrador?
The miracle of nature quickly shows,
As with the weeks and months that "handful" grows!

Note: This poem describes the litter from which we chose Tika, our yellow Labrador.

Seasonal Paralysis

Golly, gee! My goodness me!
Gosh darn it and alack!
It's gardening season once again
And Mum's put out her back.

Of course, we never doubt at all
The suffering and the pain,
But why is it always late in May
That paralysis strikes again?

She'll avoid the heavy digging
With great delight, and then
She'll be supervising which goes where
And who does what, and when!

It's surely some coincidence,
This year and many more,
That when the peas need picking
She's laid up on the floor!

We think she's just pretending
That her back is such a menace,
Except, of course, we quite forgot,
She's even given up tennis.

So, Mum, take heart, we're on your side;
Just wait a year or so...
They say most back aches cure themselves
By seventy you know!

Winter — Then and Now

Then, I was in England; a young girl growing up just after the war. Winter was gauged in Fahrenheit, and temperatures lower than fifteen were rare, but it could often feel very cold. Our house had two radiators, but no effective central heating. We walked almost everywhere, for like so many families of that time, we did not have a car.

On a cold morning, I would snuggle down in bed. The windows would be covered with miraculous, fern-like ice patterns, as if an artist had been at work while I slept. Braving the chill of my bedroom, I would dress quickly, the white cotton school blouse cold on my skin.

The milkman had finished his rounds before we were up, and the bottles outside often had ice on top. Sometimes the birds, looking for winter nourishment, had pecked through the thin silver bottle caps. My breakfast on a cold day was porridge with Tate and Lyle's Golden Syrup. If I dropped the syrup perfectly, I could see straight through it to the picture on the bottom of the bowl!

Whenever we had more than six inches of snow, I was intent on building an igloo. Once, when I was about ten, I managed to build the walls up to almost two feet. I scavenged a piece of plywood, balanced it on top, and packed on more snow. My own igloo at last!

These images are indelibly etched in my memory.

Now, I have lived in Canada, the land of real winter, for over fifty years. I hear of Celsius temperatures plunging to minus forty or so...but now we have central heating and move quickly from our heated house to our heated car!

Ten years in Terrace, British Columbia, shed some light on Canadian winters in the west. In 1971 and 1972, more than two hundred inches of snow fell. Children were urged not to climb on the snow piles, lest they should touch the power lines. We shovelled to levels above our heads.

In 1997, we visited Iqaluit, on Baffin Island, and attended a festival to mark the end of the long Arctic winter. There were demonstrations of the age-old skills of igloo building and dog sleigh driving. What a thrill it was to crawl inside a real igloo!

We still live in British Columbia – in Castlegar now. Yes, I could wish that the roads were not so icy, but when the hoar frost glistens, and the sky is blue, and the sun is shining… where else would I want to be! We love the fresh, healthy feel of the cold air and have memories of how much our dogs enjoyed the feel of the snow. We are fortunate in having neither the extended severe winter of Eastern Canada nor the damp cold of the West Coast.

Then winter was good, for I knew nothing else. *Now* it is so different, but still good, and still a season to enjoy.

Tribute and Celebration

Source of richest wisdom,
A rock in shifting sand,
An oak tree in the forest,
A trusted friend at hand.

Ever an enquiring mind,
Learning more each day;
Holding to deep convictions;
Sincere in every way.

You ran your race with honour,
Supporting those held dear;
You've moved beyond our vision
But your guiding light is clear.

We gather to remember,
To seek strength side by side,
But we also celebrate your life
With gratitude and pride.

Note: Written in memory of my father, Cecil Sainsbury, who died very suddenly on June 29th, 1989.

Happiness

Sometimes I wish
Moments could stretch to hours,
And hours then stand still.

A paradox perhaps…

For is it not the transience of joy
That gives it meaning?

A Christmas Tradition

Some of the best things that happen are unplanned! As the Christmas card season approached in 1972, I looked in sheer desperation at the list of our friends, my mother's interested friends, and our relatives on both sides. I knew I would never make it! A four-year-old, a baby, and a puppy could be blamed as the impediments to one-to-one authentic letter writing. On the other hand, forty-six years later, I think credit, rather than blame, is appropriate. After all, without their help at that crucial time, "Fleet Feats", our Christmas letter, might never have been born!

That first edition was very apologetic, as 1972 was well before duplicated Christmas letters were common. I was convinced that some of the recipients, especially my elderly relatives in England, would be totally horrified at receiving one, and I certainly never intended it to become a regular occurrence. In fact, those worries were totally unjustified, and everyone seemed to enjoy getting much more news than usual. By mistake, a grand tradition was born! I did not keep the first, desperate, hand-written letter, and a few years later, when I decided to coil bind the accumulating editions of Fleet Feats, I had to ask my father if he, by any chance, had that first copy. Fortunately, he did!

As the years have passed, technology has changed. This is reflected in the Fleet Feats booklet, which demonstrates the move from handwriting, through manual and electric typewriters, to the first computer-generated edition in 1985. Photo-copied pictures, in poor quality black and white, began to appear in 1975. Then there was the transformation to a coloured photo collage, compiled by our younger son, Jeremy, who was not even born when Fleet Feats started! For many years now, our three adult children have had the Fleet Feats booklet, and each year a new edition is added.

I have often heard criticisms of Christmas newsletters, but over the years I have had all sorts of indications of approval and even requests to, "Please keep me on your list"! I thoroughly enjoy creating the original, which often takes several days, and we always add a personal sentence or two when they are sent out. The content includes some comment about the year in general, as well as our own activities, and many times we have gone back to Fleet Feats to check on a particular date or holiday. It is a family reference resource.

For us, hearing from and communicating with our family and friends is far more important than any Christmas gifts. Fleet Feats has become a well-loved tradition, and Volume 47 will go to press this year. How long will it continue? Who knows, but it is a snatch of family history kept carefully in the archives of all the main characters. It may even be of interest to a future generation!

Perhaps...

Another time;
Another place;
Perhaps...
If paths had intertwined
We might have shared much more.

We cannot forfeit
All that we hold dear,
Or be disloyal to the ones we love...
Yet still a gentle turmoil stirs within.

Although this flowering in our lives
Cannot bear fruit,
Perhaps you find it comforting to know
That, as we both grow older,
Still you stir
A flurry of emotion
In a close friend's heart.

A Dog's Life

When planning for the future, I'll remember
Not to come back here in human form again,
But to claim reincarnation within the canine realm:
That's a lifestyle I could easily sustain!

Not just any dog, for one must be selective,
And choose with care a home and owner too,
But I would find a family where they idolized their pets,
And would do exactly what I'd have them do.

I might have to learn to like the taste of dog food,
And perhaps to take a bath just now and then;
But hearing how the children all admire me so much,
I could suffer these indignities again.

I cannot see how I'd be discontented
Just lying on the rug and running free,
And eating, and then sometimes giving comfort to my friends
As I nuzzle them and lick them lovingly.

So perhaps if you like dogs, and you outlive me,
And if reincarnation does take place,
You will see me in the future lying sprawled out on your rug
With a smile of sheer contentment on my face!

Rock

Rock lived on the top of a very high mountain. When the weather was good, he could look down in every direction and enjoy the view. He was lucky. He was a part of nature, and yet he could admire the marvels of creation all around him.

In the summer, the alpine meadows were rich with wild flowers. In the fall, Rock could see the blazing gold of tamaracks on the mountain slopes. Far below him stretched a narrow, winding lake; a mystery to Rock, but a fascination none the less. On the horizon, all around him, he could see other mountains, some so high that their tops were hidden in the clouds.

Rock felt privileged, perched on the very top of the mountain. After all, he could be half way down, looking out in only one direction. He could be hidden in a little valley or even buried deep in a cave. Good fortune had given him a position which was the envy of many.

Of course, there were some disadvantages to being at the very top of the mountain. Sometimes, when the marmots scraped away the loose stones at his feet, he began to feel a little insecure. The pressure mounted when triumphant hikers climbed all over him or even irreverently scratched their initials on his side. When the wind buffeted him relentlessly and the rain pounded him on every side, he wondered if, after all, a sheltered valley or even a cave might offer a few advantages.

Whenever Rock caught himself feeling just a little dejected, he would take a deep breath, think of the wonderful things all around him, and brave his way through the storm.

And, do you know, Rock is still there to this very day!

River of Life

River of life,
Flowing relentlessly towards its goal.

Struggling at times to keep on course;
Diminished and disheartened,
Craving replenishment from all around.

At other times in flood,
Erratic, fraught with danger;
Seeking the un-travelled path,
Sweeping away the past.

At best, in balance,
Swirling and eddying with fullness and content;
Purposeful, at peace,
Carrying its load with carefree ease;
Giving new life, nurturing...and passing on.

Quiet Miracles

High on the river bank
The morning air is damp.
A cool September mist hangs all around;
The haloed sun is slowly strengthening its resolve
And striving to unmask the earth below.

Yellowing grass and stiff, brown, knapweed stalks
Are signs that summer's glory is now gone,
But yet today this is the scene of miracles…

A sea of glistening cobwebs hanging there!

Spontaneous art, created overnight
With engineering skill and craftsman's zeal;
Displayed with elegance,
Each separate inch of web now magnified
By glistening dew drops, touching one another…

Strings of tiny pearls in morning light.

The sun gains strength,
The valley mist withdraws,
And slowly, as the warming air begins to move,
Drifting threads of gossamer will disappear.

Short-lived miracles,
Nocturnal tapestries;
A wealth of artistry for nature's purposes.

Wondering

I wonder if you ever dream
The way I dream,
And if your wandering mind traces the tracks
My mind has traced.
I wonder if you think of me
The way I think of you…
Perhaps romance is in the wondering.

O Canada!

The scene was Embetsu, a small community in the very north of Hokkaido, Japan. The date was June 21st, 1989, and the occasion, the signing of a sister-city agreement between Embetsu and Castlegar, British Columbia. There were probably about fifty people present to witness the signing ceremony, and there was an air of excitement in the small community. Everyone looked forward to the formalizing of an agreement which already existed in spirit. Six of us, including the Mayor and the President of Selkirk College, were present as representatives of Castlegar. I was there in my role as Chairperson of Selkirk College Board. Ever since our arrival, we had been treated like royalty.

As we perused the program for the ceremony, we noticed that we were to sing "O Canada". My five companions, four men and one other woman, knew that I sang in a choir, and promptly informed me that I would hold special leadership responsibility at this point. There was some rapid scribbling of what were referred to as "the new words", although they were far from recent! We knew that the Japanese are supremely comfortable singing in any circumstance, and we were just a little anxious, for there was no evidence of a music source, and when we inquired, it appeared that we were to be unaccompanied. With a background of occasionally pitching the first note for "Happy Birthday", it would be my responsibility to get us off to a good start.

When the time arrived, the singing of *O Canada* was announced in Japanese and in English. There was an expectant pause, which I interpreted as my cue. Trying not to appear too anxious, I pitched that first "O", and the rest of the group gamely joined me. We were off to a great start and had nothing to worry about...until! The surprise came as we launched into "True patriot love..." Suddenly there was music from the corner of the room! No doubt recalling the Canadian hesitancy in singing, our hosts had indeed supplied a taped accompaniment. There had simply been a misunderstanding when we asked about music and a delay in the tape starting. The problem at that point was that it was now playing the opening of the anthem just as we were gaining our confidence on the second line!

Perhaps we missed our chance to experiment with "O Canada" in canon form, but discretion seemed the better part of valour. Much humbled, we adjusted our pitch, and our words, and attempted to redeem ourselves. The good news is that the sister-city agreement, which for the last twenty years has included a student exchange program, is still flourishing almost thirty years later!

Changing Seasons

Autumn lingers; winter hesitates.
November air is fresh,
Summer-green grass is faded now,
And just a few reluctant leaves
Cling stiffly on to gaunt, brown branches.

The aspen stand on guard,
Stark silhouettes against an ominous sky.
Graceful birches, now disrobed for sleep,
Ease the sombre tones with silver-white,
And huddling close on mountain slopes
Are pines and firs, their brilliant spring-green tips
Now darkened in disguise,
To hide themselves from winter's bleak advance.

In flower beds the faded marigolds stand
As monuments to summer's recent splendour.
The fallen leaves are raked,
And garden earth lies bare and brown,
Summer's lush harvest but a distant memory.
In daring contrast to this sombre mood
Bright orange pyracantha berries mass,
As if defying nature's age-old lore.

Clouds rest lazily on neighbouring mountains,
Now and then lifting to unveil
Visions of winter's new-found mantle, dazzling white.
A few procrastinating birds gather their strength
To face the wearying journey south.

It is as if the earth is pausing, taking breath,
Before it plunges into depths of winter sleep.

A Gentle Message

We did not touch,
Or speak of closeness
Which we knew was ours.

Friendship's bond was seemingly carefree,
As if there was no stirring deep within.

Yet in those special days,
The quietness was eloquence itself:
Hints of tender caring
Bridged the gulf of silence
And transcended words...
A gentle message; gently understood.

Old Glory

"Old Glory" is a mountain close to the skiing community of Rossland, in British Columbia. It is the highest peak in the southern Monashee Range. The first time Terry and I climbed to the top was in 1995, and it was a memorable occasion!

I had looked so often at Old Glory, both from the road near Nancy Greene Lake, and from the air, when flying in or out of Castlegar. The long ridge, which slowly rises to the highest point, ends with a precipitous drop off. An old fire lookout is perched at the summit.

It was August, and we wanted to take on a new hiking challenge! The weekend weather forecast had not been particularly good, but we decided that, if it was reasonable on the Saturday morning, we would set out towards Old Glory. We would have open minds and be willing to turn back at any stage. The hiking trail starts eleven kilometres from Rossland, on the road to Nancy Greene Lake, and it goes up and up, through sub-alpine forests of cedar and hemlock. We passed through all the phases of huckleberries; they were over at the bottom, at their prime about 2 kilometres into the hike, and still tiny and green as we broke out of the forest at the tree line. It was a steep and often rocky trail, rather like climbing up a river bed much of the time, but the huckleberries helped us forge on! This part of the hike ends at Unnecessary Ridge, and by then we were already seeing magnificent displays of alpine wild flowers: Indian paintbrush, lupins, arnica, valerian, and so many others.

That first part of the climb took us two hours and we gained about 2000 feet. The weather was still in our favour as we looked across the valley towards Old Glory, and mountain goats beckoned from the cliffs near the summit!

Unnecessary Ridge is so named because one has immediately to descend about 400 feet and then re-climb it, which is very frustrating! It took us another hour and twenty minutes to get up to the summit, first going down and across the basin, then up the long, slow gradient

85

leading to the lower end of the ridge, and finally another half hour or so making our way up to the top.

It was during that last stretch that we became increasingly aware of storm clouds moving in rather quickly from the west. The wind had picked up, and it even hailed a little before we reached the summit, but there was still lots of blue sky. We reached the fire lookout which was boarded up and padlocked at that time. It is a small building perched precariously on the rocky peak, with little room for anything else, including people! We had gained another thousand feet since Unnecessary Ridge, and both Terry and I were quite affected by the drop offs on three sides of us. The summit is slightly under 8000 feet, and the precipice at the northern end drops several hundred feet.

We enjoyed a great sense of triumph but did not even spend five minutes at the top! The looming clouds had grown closer, the hail had started again, and the wind was blowing even harder. We left in a hurry, but with great care, anxious to get off the main ridge. It was a shame that we could not sit in the flowers somewhere and enjoy our lunch, but when everything around is wet, and thunder is rolling ominously, the only sensible thing to do is to seek safety!

By the time we had descended to the basin, the thunder and lightning seemed to be right over the summit; exactly where we had been about an hour before! We were so glad to be in a less exposed location. I had never before seen lightning and heard thunder simultaneously, and the echoes in the mountains made it even more impressive…but very alarming! By the time we got back to Unnecessary Ridge, the hail had turned to snow, the whole of Old Glory was in cloud, and the thunder was still rolling!

There was a certain novelty in watching August snowflakes land on the brightly coloured flowers, and we did pause long enough to take a couple of pictures. Our legs and hands were cold, but we had good jackets with hoods. I did regret not bringing gloves, but when packing in midsummer they are not one's first thought!

It was another six kilometres from Unnecessary Ridge back to the car. As we moved down, it was snowing hard, our boots had soaked through, and our jackets were dripping down our legs. The snow turned to heavy rain as we moved into the forest. The trail was quite definite, but overgrown with lush alder growth, dripping before we even touched it! Any part of us that was dry got wet from pushing our way through, and it really made no difference if we walked through deep puddles at this stage. We would have been quite a vision if there had been anyone else around, but there was not, and we could at least see a humorous side in our situation!

It took us about three hours to get down from the summit. If we had not known exactly where the trail was, it would have been a worry, but as it was, we were wet, and a little cold, but otherwise fine. The enjoyment of the morning had been well worth the discomfort of the downward trek in the afternoon. The hot coffee in Rossland was welcome, and it was not long before we were speeding home.

Back at the house, we squeezed the water out of our socks, enjoyed a hot shower, and were none the worse for our experience. We were pleased to have climbed Old Glory; our choice of weather could have been better, but special memories were created!

Note: We have climbed Old Glory three times since that first experience, most recently in 2017. It is not an easy hike, but it has never again been the challenge that it was that first time.

Hiromi and Friends

They were as little boats,
Tossing in an unknown sea;
Separated, fragile and unsure.
Their faces held some fleeting hints of joy,
But all around was strange,
And language lost.

With passing days, the seas appeared to calm,
And new and lasting smiles were quickly seen.
The waves brought fear no more,
And soon with confidence
Each tiny vessel made its way to shore.

Close bonds of friendship formed;
For two short weeks
We shared our lives.
The deepest form of human language thrived:
The smiles, the bonds of fellowship and love,
The shared excitements and the parting tears;
For these emotions words are not enough.

Now, as the tree of friendship takes its root,
We see a spark of hope for days ahead:
The open arms of love and understanding
Can help to soothe all fears,
And, as we learn from others and enrich our lives,
So, in a subtle way, will grow
Fresh understanding in this world of ours.

Note: Hiromi was a Japanese student who stayed with us for two weeks in 1987.

Silence

Two minds mingle in silence:
Thoughts unspoken,
Feelings unexpressed.

Two souls in harmony:
No words are heard,
But all is understood.

In Appreciation

Tradition, without a soul, is sterile;
Dry bones, ranged in ordered rows,
Yet lacking life.

It's true that we were ready, right on cue...

The grass was cut,
Red carpets all laid out,
Musicians well-rehearsed...

We knew our role.

All was in order,
Lacking only an inspiration
Which could give meaning
To this well-staged exercise.

Your warmth and caring and your understanding way,
The touching words and anecdotes from life,
Revealed two souls at peace within their lives,
Imparting a calmness and tranquillity.

We valued the sincerity you showed;
Lessons passed on...
You've been accepted in the years gone by,
And in devoted service, now,
Offer your contribution in return.

Time, then, in preparation
Had been all well spent...
Tradition enhanced, gave splendour to routine;
Showed itself worthy of the respect we'd paid...
Yet, of itself, could not have won the day.

Note: This poem was written for British Columbia's former Lieutenant Governor, The Honourable David C. Lam, and Her Honour Mrs. Dorothy Lam. It recalls the occasion of their visit to Selkirk College on June 1ˢᵗ, 1990.

Our "Best Friends"

From childhood, I had always wanted a dog. My parents were given a dog when they were married in 1934. I was born in 1943, and by the time I could take Garm for walks, he could barely walk at all. I loved my uncle's dogs, Gretel, Scamp, Bimbo... I could name all the dogs on our road, Roddy, Tuppy, Amber, Monty... I looked forward to the times when a friend of my mother's left Smuts, and subsequently Marcus, with us for a few days – but I really longed for a dog of my own.

When Terry and I had been married for four years, in 1972, the opportunity finally came. Friends of ours had bred their German short-haired pointer with a Labrador, and we were to have one of the pups. We called our family addition "Liska". Perhaps there was a Labrador somewhere in her, but she had the long, lean, freckled look of a pointer, and in this way matched one of her owners in the uncanny way that dogs often do.

A short time after Liska joined us, in the raging August heat of a non-airconditioned house, she became very fussy in the night. Terry, on the second or third wake-up call, moved her outside with more vigour than he intended. Then the real problem began! The next day at the vet's, we were told that Liska had a hairline crack in a bone and needed to be kept very quiet for a few weeks. Graham was three years old and Jane only six months at the time, and we decided that the only chance of suppressing the movement of a three-month-old dog consistently would be for her to stay with the vet. It was an expensive start to dog ownership, but she survived, and so did we.

At a remarkably young age, Liska could be seen in "point" position: front leg lifted and bent, and tail held straight. Terry did occasionally take her out hunting, and she quite possibly had the potential to be a useful aid, but our commitments with a young family did not allow for the necessary training time and energy. For our own sanity at home, we did train Liska to stay on her mat when she was in the living room. The only time I ever heard a minor growl from her was when Jeremy, not appreciating her very limited bounds, crawled onto her mat and occupied her only space!

When we moved from Terrace to Castlegar in 1980, Liska was to fly with us in a crate in the hold. On the vet's suggestion, we had tranquillized her, and we all left on the plane together, heading to Prince Rupert and then on to Vancouver. All was well until a door on the plane would not close properly in preparation for take-off from Prince Rupert. After considerable delays, we were informed that another plane was being sent from Vancouver and ours was to be unloaded. Poor Liska – when we took her out of her crate, she was so wobbly, and of course by the time the replacement plane arrived, she was bright-eyed and raring to go, which was not what we intended. Liska was our friend and companion for 13 years, leaving us in 1985.

Our next dog was Tika, a yellow Labrador first seen by all the family when she was only hours old. When she joined us a few weeks later, it was hard not to spoil her. Our children were older, and we relented on the mat issue and let her go anywhere downstairs, but not on the furniture. In thunderstorms, if we were upstairs, she would try to make herself look small and slink up the stairs, tail between legs, to join us and find comfort.

Tika was a wonderful dog, and in 1990 we decided that we would let her have just one litter of puppies. Her mate was another good looking, purebred, yellow Labrador, and, as genetics books will tell you, if you mate a yellow Lab with another yellow Lab, you will by some quirk of nature always have a litter of all yellow puppies, regardless of any recessive black or chocolate genes. Tika was a devoted mother to ten offspring, and we found it an amazing study in sociology watching their little characters develop. Some puppies will literally crawl over the top of others to feed; others will hang back, as if they know they cannot compete and might as well wait their turn. It was all lots of work, but the neighbourhood children were quite thrilled to come and see the puppies almost every afternoon on the front lawn.

It was a time when yellow Labradors were much in demand, and to our surprise, we found ourselves quite keen for Tika to repeat the event. In 1991, she had her second litter. Her mate that time was a chocolate

Lab, and quite surprisingly, we found ourselves with five black puppies and four yellow. Again, we watched with interest as the puppies opened their eyes at two weeks and slowly developed their distinct characteristics. In the evenings, we would watch a column of little dogs make their way to the door, spend time on the grass, and then come back in. Only once did we make the mistake of not watching well enough. It is easy for a small puppy to squeeze between the pickets of a fence, and it is rather alarming looking for a missing, very small, black dog in the dark!

Tika lived to be almost sixteen years old, and it was devastating saying goodbye to her. She was everyone's friend, and many of our neighbours had shared dog duties at various times.

Sally, our last dog, was inherited from friends of ours in Calgary. She was a chocolate Lab and already four years old when she came to us. She had some hip problems and had to be kept from playing roughly with other dogs. Our friends were told she would do well with an "elderly" couple. We were not so sure that epithet fitted us, since we were still in our fifties, but names mean nothing, and we once again had a delightful dog who nuzzled her way into our hearts.

The neighbours loved Sally too, and at age 12, in the summer of 2008, she hosted a barbecue to thank all the friends who helped us in looking after her. Then, within a month, she was gone, having apparently suffered a stroke.

So ended, for the time being, our thirty-six years of dog ownership. I stress, "for the time being"! Jeremy still says that the house does not seem right without a dog, and my childhood craving will probably never be satisfied. We may have to wait until we are not travelling so much, and we may have to choose a smaller breed, but we have still kept all the necessities for another "best friend"!

The Grapevine

"Have you heard?"
"Did you know?"
"Is it true?"
"That can't be so!"

"You must be wrong –
I know for sure
From friends who know
The folks next door!"

"Don't say a word –
I shouldn't tell!"
"My lips are closed –
All will be well."

"Have you heard?"
"Did you know?"
"I never did!"
"That can't be so!"

Gossiping?
Who?
Me?

On Leaving Embetsu

We remember many faces,
And many different smiles;
The people of Embetsu
Stay with us through the miles.

Friends we have just discovered
Yet have to leave behind,
With their deep concern and caring:
Gracious, welcoming, and kind.

The seeds of peace are planted;
In time they yield their fruit.
The ties of understanding grow;
New friendships now take root.

Our cities seek the unity
Which we've found on our way.
May they grow in fellowship and peace,
United more each day.

Note: A Castlegar delegation stayed in Embetsu, Japan for the signing of a Sister City agreement on June 21st, 1989.

Shining Forever

Stars shine on,
Through day and night,
But are not always seen.

Moments of joy within our lives
May pass behind the clouds;

But still remain…
Forever…

Live on within our souls.

A Favourite Escape Trail

An inauspicious beginning: a gravel pit and composting area on the left and a one-train-a-day train track on the right. Who could think of this as an escape…yet it is the beginning of a hidden gem for those who enjoy watching the change of seasons reflected day by day in nature.

This trail begins just behind the Castlegar Recreation Complex. Once past the gravelled area, there are wonderful views over the Columbia River, flowing about two hundred feet below. A variety of bushes, trees, and wildflowers border the trail, and part way along one can branch down on a smaller path all the way to the water. We have enjoyed watching beavers and river otters there, just twenty minutes' walk from our home.

Dog walkers in plenty enjoy this escape into non-leash country, but sometimes one sees no one. In the winter, the way is never officially cleared, yet the constant tread of the trail loyalists keeps it passable, even when there is more than a foot of snow. Cross-country skiers some-times pass through and the occasional snowmobile. There is no ordinary vehicle access as the trail is gated at one end and blocked off by chal-lenging concrete barriers at the other.

Our dogs may have thought of this as their trail. This is where they met new friends: Aspen, Tam, Brodie, Spud, and others. To this day, we often know the dogs' names, but not their owners'. We greet each other smilingly and pass on. A common bond between us ensures that when the occasional party people leave litter in their wake, it is quickly gath-ered by those who follow.

Another source of our enjoyment of the trail is that it has taught us to appreciate the orderly sequence of nature. The early blossoms of Oregon grape, choke cherry and Saskatoon berry are followed, accord-ing to pre-ordained plan, by wild roses, Columbian lilies, syringa, and ocean spray, to name a few. In the fall, the dried stems of knapweed are often made glorious by cobwebs, glistening with dew. Even in the patchy grass around the gravel pit, one can admire the frolics of killdeer and those tiny balls of fluff that are their young.

More than twenty years ago, our family built a small wooden bench and placed it in a beautiful position overlooking the river. It was a retreat place from which to watch the bald eagles and ospreys and to admire the magnificence of the river and the mountains. Less appreciative individuals have occasionally toppled the bench down the bank or assaulted it with graffiti. We have rescued it or repainted it ourselves many times, but sometimes it has been put back in place by others whom we do not even know. The bushes and trees all around have grown so much now that the stopping point is more like a sanctuary than a viewpoint. In the very hot weather, it is a marvellous, shady retreat.

We often like to escape to the grandeur of the mountains, but every day we wonder at the magnificence of nature right on our own doorstep. Absolute beauty is there…if we can only slow the frenetic pace and take pleasure in it.

Always With Us

Age has brought beauty with serenity;
We never hear you complain.
You forget the testing years, the suffering,
And simply claim
That life has treated you well.

Your smile is one of warmth and tenderness,
Concealing the cares you often feel within.
You touch the hearts of many,
And scatter your love
Without a thought of gain.

Too often, those who mean most to us are gone,
Not knowing their worth.
You journey far, but yet you still are close;
For, always know,
How deeply you are held within our hearts.

Note: Written for, and shared with, my mother, Ivy Sainsbury, just before her return
to England in January 1990.

First Robin

Why was he here alone?

"Early March," they had told him;
That's what he remembered.
"Early March will be fine –
You can be sure of that!"

And yet he felt that, somehow, he'd been duped.
Why was this such a good idea for him,
But not for others on their northward flight?

He fluffed indignant feathers against the cold,
Forlornly longing to shrink his shivering form
And be unnoticed...
As one falling leaf...
Or as a single star, 'midst thousands in the sky.

Resentfully he hopped through falling snow,
As if in disbelief,
Then perched his fluffed-up bulk upon the fence
To contemplate the dreary winter scene.

A figure, at a window, briefly glimpsed,
But all was quiet...
Perhaps he was not noticed after all,
And none had sensed the incongruity!

Quietly he would endure this reproach,
Then pass those same words on...
Ensuring there would be, another year,
A new and unsuspecting pioneer!

The Fox Cardigan

In 1995, Mother finally decided that she could no longer cope with the house and large garden that had been her home in England since 1934. She decided to move into a retirement home in a pleasant rural area close by. At Christmas that year, however, she followed through on her plans to come and stay with our family in Castlegar, coping with all the inconveniences of trans-Atlantic air travel on her own at age 89! She and Father had loved Christmases in Canada, and she was not about to give them up. The following year, my husband and I made our plans to go to England for her ninetieth birthday.

There is always the dilemma of finding an appropriate gift for an elderly person when clothes and possessions have already been drastically reduced in the move to a care home. My mother *needed* nothing. In the end, we gave her current photographs of our family, some flowers, and some of her favourite Purdy's dark-chocolate ginger. She had a wonderful party and was very happy. Her most significant gift, however, came from dear friends of ours who were not part of our family, but who have taught me a great deal.

My parents were not rich, but my mother always managed to look elegant. She loved clothes and seemed to know exactly what suited her. When she moved into her one room at the retirement home, it was hard for her to reduce her wardrobe. She had lived through the war and hated to throw things away if they still had "wear" in them.

Amongst the clothing that one might give to an elderly person, the first things that come to mind are dressing gowns and bedroom slippers. Along with a few day clothes, what else could one possibly need? While there was a tendency for most of those invited to the ninetieth birthday celebration to focus on what my mother *needed* or *didn't need,* our friends, Gillian and Hugh, thought of what my mother might *like.* Quite possibly the most welcome present that she received for her birthday was their gift of a beautiful, new, hip-length knitted cardigan, with red foxes prominent in the design. She loved it and always wore it with such pleasure and pride.

We all like a change now and again! The fox cardigan was such a special lesson to me. It was a reminder to think of what might bring pleasure to an older person; to think of older people as truly living and not simply waiting for that next stage.

On Labour Day of 2000 my mother died. She was almost 94, and at her funeral we listened to many wonderful tributes. Most of her clothes had already been disposed of before my husband and I arrived from Canada, but still remaining was the fox cardigan. I had seen the identical garment in a shop in Victoria and had been quite tempted at that time. Now, the cardigan was mine if I wanted it. I unhesitatingly brought it home with me, and it now hangs in my hall closet awaiting spring weather. It is such a good feeling to put on something which I know made my mother so happy, and I almost feel that a part of her is with me when I wear it.

Recollections

A phrase recalled;
A tone of voice;
A smile perhaps...
Imprinted in the memory.

The hemlocks in the spring;
The osprey's nest...

Glimpses of the past,
Held close within.

Last Day

Moving on,
Breaking the workplace ties,
Leaving the empty office where your papers were lately strewn.

Taking the pictures down,
Packing the files and books,
Clearing the shelves of trophies and of notes;
Passing the triumphs and struggles to another.

Relief from the daunting pace, moments to reflect;
A touch of sadness every now and then...
But looking round and listening to the words of adulation,
The greatest sense is satisfaction.
So much has been achieved;
Accomplishments remain and so do friends.

Slowly the book is closing,
Yours the contentment of a job well done.

As morning comes from night, as life moves on,
Last day leads on to first of what comes next.
Apprehension and excitement blend;
New ideas take form,
New paths to take, grounded in your success.

Move on with thanks and praise, voiced and unvoiced,
Knowing the caring that your friends convey.
Create a future which fulfills your dreams,
Yet guards a place to treasure memories.

Note: Written for Dr. Leo Perra's last day of his twenty years as President of Selkirk College – June 28th, 2000.

A Summer Evening in Victoria

The sun softens to a gentle evening glow;
The inner harbour lies at peace once more.

Vessels of all descriptions take their rest:
Self-conscious funnelled ferry, towering high,
Looks on his smaller berth-mates quizzically.
Exclusive sailboats bob in confidence,
Ignoring the veteran fishing schooner's gaze.
The float plane, though no longer ostracized,
Still stands apart as if to earn his rank.

And all this time insistent seagulls scream,
Telling their tales in raucous harmony,
Yet adding to this scene an elegance
As they soar with effortless grace in calm, clear air.

People of different colours, races, creeds,
Wander at leisure round the harbour's edge.
Contrasting sounds of street musicians merge:
Accordion, then haunting oboe strains –
The music rendered with a heart-felt joy,
As if reward were of no consequence.

Buildings with different histories blend in peace:
Museum's angled beauty now at ease
Beside the green-domed stately seat of power;
The ivy-clad hotel, which once disdained
Each new arrival as it took its place;
The Roman-pillared steam ship terminal,
Revived now for a different role…
All these and others merge contentedly;
Historic backdrop for the stage today.

Busy point of entry and of exit,
Thronged by tourists from all walks of life;
A gentle place, well cared for and unspoiled;
Rare source of peace amidst a world of strife.
This haven in the storms of daily living
At other times less tranquil will appear,
But as a peaceful August evening passes,
All that the world can offer now is here.

A Birthday Ode!

Kitchener, your birthplace,
Seventy years ago;
You started life there, but your folks
Soon left Ontario.

Just seven when the Queen was crowned --
In England for a while;
And then in France and Belgium
Just to start your life in style.

Back to Ontario you came;
Tobacco fields and more.
Then to the base in Winnipeg;
Dish washing was your chore.

At age 16, you'd had enough;
Went north and joined The Bay.
For two years learned to deal in furs…
And other skills I'd say!

With sense enough to finish school,
To Kamloops on you journeyed;
Then lab work at Prince Rupert mill,
Where love your course determined…

A special friend lived just downstairs –
The rest is history:
Prince Rupert, Terrace, Castlegar,
And now you're seventy!

Loved for kindness to young and old,
Family and friends for sure,
We're gathered now to raise a glass
To your next decade and more!

Note: Written for the celebration of Terry Fleet's 70th birthday on May 9th, 2016.

"Nothing Ventured, Nothing Gained!"

Immigrants to Canada in the eighteenth or nineteenth centuries might never see their families again, and if they received any news, it was usually months out of date. In order to settle satisfactorily in a strange land, it was often best to try to forget the family they had left behind.

Fortunately, things had changed a great deal by the mid-twentieth century. I was always able to keep in touch with my family and to maintain a feeling of belonging. I also kept my curiosity about certain aspects of our family history, and in 2013, when Terry and I were planning a trip to New Zealand, "the disappearing Uncle Frank" came to my mind once again. It was a mystery which had even haunted my mother. Perhaps, almost a hundred years after the event, there was a chance of finding the solution.

Uncle Frank, the oldest of eight children, was born in 1887. My mother, Ivy Pettengell, was the youngest in the family, born in 1906. The only thing that she ever said about Uncle Frank, when my brothers and I were growing up, went something like this:

"Well, he went off to New Zealand after the First World War, and no one ever heard from him again. Perhaps he was killed in the great earthquake."

When I was visiting Mother, following my father's death in 1989, she revealed a little more information to me. Uncle Frank had been born before my grandparents were married; in the words of the time he was "a bastard". At age 18, Thomas Pettengell, my grandfather, was suddenly sent off to California "to learn fruit farming". Meanwhile house maid Elizabeth Nunn, my grandmother, gave birth to Francis, our Uncle Frank.

After two years of "fruit farming", Thomas Pettengell returned to England and married Elizabeth Nunn. They had seven more children, and Frank, having spent his early childhood with his mother's parents, did eventually move to the Pettengells' house, but he was never given the family name. On his birth certificate he was listed as "Francis Nunn -- father unknown", but Mother spoke as if the siblings all knew he was their full brother. Frank fought in World War I and then emigrated to New Zealand in 1922. Mother thought he was seeking a new life there, perhaps because he was never really treated as one of the family. No one ever heard from him after that.

In 2013, when I was planning our New Zealand holiday, the mystery of Uncle Frank's disappearance was constantly in my mind. He was a close relative; my mother's brother. Was he really killed, or did I by any chance have cousins in New Zealand? There *was* an earthquake in New Zealand in 1931, and 250 people *were* killed, but that was nine years after Frank left England, and no one had heard from him during that time.

It seemed unlikely that the mystery could be solved after almost a hundred years, but, remembering the expression, "Nothing ventured, nothing gained," I perused the New Zealand White Pages on the computer and there were 67 Nunns listed. Unfortunately no e-mail addresses were available, and the cost of postage would be considerable. I suggested to Terry that the expenditure might be considered an "investment" if it were successful, as it could possibly add to the interest and enjoyment of our holiday! In April 2013, I sent letters of enquiry to 29 of the listed individuals. The letter was carefully worded, giving the required amount of family background, and simply asking if anyone knew of a Francis Nunn, born in 1887, in their family. I selected the addresses strategically, covering several towns and cities in the country to maximize my chances.

I received three well-wishing replies from people who were clearly not related to me. Then came the very special e-mail from Natalie Nunn. It was one of those "heart stopping" moments when I read what she had written,

"My grandfather's name *was* Francis Nunn."

Natalie had a copy of her grandfather's birth certificate and had sent for her own father's birth certificate too, just to be sure. In June, when the confirming document arrived, we all discovered that she and her three sisters are indeed blood relatives of mine, our common ancestor quite certainly being my grandmother…and almost certainly my grandfather too! We are first cousins, one generation removed.

Natalie and I conversed by e-mail several times in the next few months, and then, in February 2014, Terry and I flew to New Zealand for our holiday. We were greeted by Natalie and her two boys at Auckland Airport, and a few days later we were invited to a family gathering at cousin Margaret's house. It was quite amazing to walk into a room surrounded by smiling, welcoming people who were newly discovered close relatives! Near the end of our holiday, Natalie, her boys, and two of her sisters spent time with us at Whanganui, the city where Uncle Frank had settled and raised his family. We saw where he lived, the memorial to his wife Lily, where his ashes were scattered, and a 1959 newspaper tribute remembering "Whanganui's first bus driver". Since that time, cousin Alison and her husband Stuart have also visited us in Canada.

Uncle Frank did not "die in the great earthquake"! He lived successfully in New Zealand, drove a bus for many years, had a family and a dairy farm in Whanganui, and was well respected. I wished my mother had known this, but I am sure she would have been pleased that we solved the mystery. We met three of Uncle Frank's four granddaughters, all charming people, and this added special meaning to what was already an incredible holiday.

Operating on the principle of "Nothing ventured, nothing gained!" was surprisingly worthwhile. I tried, and it worked! The truly amazing aspect of the story is that Natalie had chosen not to change her maiden name "Nunn" when she married. If she had made a different choice our enquiring letter would never have reached her!

And Sometimes...Magic

Special times;
The flowers in our lives.

Favourite places;
Scenes of happiness.

Treasured moments;
Memories of joy.

Unspoken messages...
And sometimes...magic.

Tapestry

The tapestry of life evolves
Slowly through the years;
Each joy, each pain recorded,
And worked with smiles or tears.
Events, once so important,
Standing on their own,
In the end close-blending
And merging into one.

As we work the grand designs,
And see things close at hand,
A glimpse of beauty, now and then,
Can help us understand
That even failings and mistakes,
And false paths we have traced,
Are threaded in the master plan
As if with purpose placed.

Woven in the tapestry,
With tenderness and care,
Are hints of those held dear to us,
Whose dreams and hopes we've shared.
Joys of the present and the past
Amidst life's turmoil shine;
The mystery of the future
Will complete the grand design.

Awakening

The sky is blue, with wispy wind–drawn clouds;
The morning sunlight glows on rocks and trees;
The hillside meld of tired winter browns
Is scattered here and there with hints of green,
As waking birch and aspen groves
Are lured to spring-time sun.

Swollen buds are bursting with new life;
The warm wind softly strokes green tips of pines
And delicate emerald lace of hemlock boughs.

New life abounds;
Winter's time of doubt has passed,
And spirits are reborn.

Closing the Circle

Perhaps I foresaw my destiny in Canada at an early age. When I was only nine and had to write about a country of my choice, I chose Canada. At my father's suggestion, I even wrote to the Canadian Embassy in London for information. In 1958, when I was fifteen, I purchased a book with glorious coloured photographs, entitled *Land of the Long Day*. It was written by Doug Wilkinson and described his experiences when he spent a year with the "Eskimos" in Pond Inlet, Baffin Island.

Eight years later, in 1966, I made the decision to work in Canada for two years. As I packed my belongings, I included the Wilkinson book. I was not heading to Baffin Island, and I did not anticipate really needing it, but it was the only book about Canada that I owned.

Fast forward thirty years to 1996! *Land of the Long Day* had sat benevolently on my bookcase and had only very occasionally been taken down. By this time, Terry and I were well established in Castlegar, and our three children were all at university or working. Our daughter Jane, who was training as a doctor, was coming to the end of her two-year residency in Ottawa. Incredible as it may now seem, there was not a great need for general practitioners in Canada at that time, and she was a little anxious about where she would be working the following year. She intimated to us that she might have to go to the United States.

By 1996, only the two of us were living in our house in Castlegar, and I was making great efforts to sort through the household posses-sions and sensibly dispose of things that were not needed. In the realm of books, I had a sentimental look at *Land of the Long Day* but became more ruthless when I thought of how infrequently it had been taken from the shelf in recent years. Into the box it went, heading for the second-hand bookshop.

Just two weeks after that, Jane phoned to let us know that she *would* be working in Canada the following year; she had a position in Baffin Island. My immediate thought was, "But I've given away the book!" I made three visits to the second-hand bookshop in the next few weeks,

and finally found *Land of the Long Day* on the Canadiana shelf. I humbly bought it again for two dollars, laminated the cover, took it home, and lovingly restored it to the shelf!

We visited Jane in Iqaluit in 1997, but it was far too expensive to go on to Pond Inlet, and we were more than satisfied exploring in the Iqaluit and Pangnirtung areas. Twelve years later, however, in 2009, Jane and her husband were again in Baffin Island with their one son, Michael. They were expecting their second child, and Terry and I planned to visit shortly after the birth.

Jane knew of my intense interest in Pond Inlet and had been there herself as a locum. While we were planning our trip, she suggested that we use air travel points to go up to Pond Inlet for a weekend. It was almost too good to be true that we also had a close friend in Castlegar whose son was teaching there and who offered us his apartment as he would be away at the time. The stars were all aligned, it seemed, and our plans were made. With no real expectation that it would be needed, I put *Land of the Long Day* in my suitcase and even prepared a little plaque for the inside cover…just in case!

We spent a few days in Iqaluit with Jane and family and gave an appropriate welcome to William, our new grandson. Then, on a Friday afternoon, we set off to Pond Inlet, which is now a community of approximately 1500 people, almost all of whom are Inuit. It is situated 600 kilometres inside the Arctic Circle at 72°N. We were on separate airlines, as only one "free" seat was available on each flight, but we both arrived safely.

We had arranged to go for a hike the next morning, accompanied by a seventeen-year-old Inuit student, Adrian, who would carry a high-powered rifle. A polar bear encounter was very unlikely, but a possibility. At nine o'clock, Adrian arrived at the apartment with his grandma, Regilee Ootova. She and I started talking for a short time, and I showed her the book. I turned to a picture page where there were several close-ups of people from the community. Doug Wilkinson's year in Pond Inlet had commenced in 1953, and 56 years later I was asking Adrian's grandma if she recognized anyone! What were the chances?!

"Oh yes," she said. "This person is still alive, and the little baby is Mary Krimmerdjuak. If you go to church tomorrow, you could meet her."

We hiked with Adrian for most of the day and saw magnificent scenery across ice-rimmed Eclipse Sound. Back in Pond Inlet, we walked around town again, and later that night took a blue sky and sunshine picture right at midnight. The sun was shining down on us straight from the north; it was an incredible experience!

The next morning, we attended the Anglican church service, guessing at what was happening, as it was entirely in Inuktitut! After the service we had a fascinating chat with "Mary", who obviously had no memories of Doug Wilkinson's project, as she was only months old at the time. She, and others, were more than willing to sign the little plaque I had made, giving their names in syllabics and in English. Mary even wrote in the page number of her picture and was quite thrilled about it all.

Later that day, we met with Philippa Ootoowak, the community archivist. She showed us Doug Wilkinson's original photographs. She also mentioned that Wilkinson had been very much respected by the Inuit. He had died the previous year and a special memorial was held for him. Philippa had originally come from England, as a nurse. She arrived in Pond Inlet in 1973, eventually married an Inuk, learned to speak the language, and raised her family there… and I thought that going to Prince Rupert was adventurous!

After our special weekend in Pond Inlet, we returned to Iqaluit, on our separate planes! Terry went via Igloolik, and I had a two-and-a-half-hour direct flight, looking down over the ice caps, glaciers, and other Arctic scenery. We enjoyed a few more days with Jane and family before leaving Baffin Island. Meeting William and helping Jane had been our original focus, but the trip to Pond Inlet was another real highlight, not just of the holiday, but of my life. It felt as if I was closing a circle, and my book had made its way "home"!

On Entering a New Year

Reluctantly we read the final chapter of a well-loved book;
We see, complete, the web of mystery or intrigue;
No questions left unanswered, all resolved.
We are well satisfied,
Yet sever the ties with sorrow, eager to read on.

And with the closing of a year?

If scarred with sadness, it is willingly put by;
We scan the final words in haste, endeavouring to forget.
If pleasure-filled, we think back sentimentally,
And relish each happy chapter, line by line:
It was a year well spent,
And put aside with gentle reverence...

But here the likeness ends.

Our lives progress from year to year.
We treasure the memories, or reject them,
But each old year leaves questions unresolved:
What happiness and sadness lie ahead?

Passing embraces and good wishes mark
One tiny watershed of many in our lives.
The years resemble marshalled runners, taking turns;
At midnight the torch is passed from
one hand to the next...

And life goes on....

Notes

On Watch at Victoria Harbour

The comparisons in this poem are between the representations of Captain Vancouver on top of the Legislative Building, Queen Victoria on the lawn outside, and Captain Cook, who does indeed look "straight at the Empress Hotel"!

Ode to a Welshman

For a church fundraiser, I offered to write short poems to celebrate special days or events. Terry and I went to people's houses dressed in clown costumes for the presentations. This poem, and the leek, were presented to Deon Miskell on St. David's Day, March 1st, 1991. "Cymru Am Byth" means "Wales for ever."

Travelling

The reference to "Ships that pass in the night" is from the poem *Tales of a Wayside Inn* by Longfellow:

"Ships that pass in the night, and speak each other in passing:
Only a signal shown and a distant voice in the darkness,
So on the ocean of life we pass and speak one another,
Only a look and a voice; then darkness again and a silence.

From a Hotel Window

This poem had its origins when I was looking down from the 14th floor of the Sutton Place Hotel in Vancouver. I was waiting for a meeting and watching people make their way to work. They looked like "scurrying ants"!

Early Morning by the Lake
This selection was written just prior to a Selkirk College Board retreat. I had recently been elected as Chairperson, and I knew that contentious issues would be coming up.

Waiting by the Lake
Friends were cross-country skiing around Nancy Greene Lake. I was having back trouble at the time and waiting for them in the log hut.

A Silent Birth
This poem reflects on the birth of our stillborn daughter on August 24th, 1973. It is a date I still remember every year.

The Touch of Love
This selection had its genesis as I held the hand of Marjorie Williams, our neighbour, when she lay dying in the hospital in 1991. Marjorie was a loving "third grandmother" for our children and a mentor for me.

Metamorphosis
This piece was written when our daughter was in her mid-teens. Adolescence is very comparable to the metamorphosis of a caterpillar into a butterfly.

Separation
This was written when contemplating the withdrawal from parents that occurs as an adolescent seeks independence.

Change
Change is often a challenge, and this poem is easily understood in a generic way. I was actually reflecting on the end of my nine years on the Selkirk College Board.

Seasonal Paralysis

This poem was written in 1987. Now I know for sure that back problems do not actually "disappear at 70", but I am better at preventing them from occurring!

Rock

I served for four years as Chairperson of Selkirk College Board. I was also President of the Advanced Education Council of British Columbia for two years. In both of those positions, there were times when "half way down the mountain" or "hidden in a cave" seemed quite appealing!

In Appreciation

Dr. Lam loved poetry. This poem was subsequently published (in Chinese) in his biography. I spent a delightful time at Government House in Victoria, reading poems at his request.

On Leaving Embetsu

This poem was written on the bus as we left Embetsu to travel to Sapporo. It was subsequently translated into Japanese and hangs in Embetsu City Hall.

First Robin

This really did happen. The fluffed up robin looked most indignant, sitting on our back fence. I observed from the kitchen window and was the "figure briefly glimpsed". I did not know at the time that some robins do in fact stay around all winter.

A Birthday Ode

In Prince Rupert, when we first met, Terry boarded at the house where I shared a basement suite with another English teacher. There were three other boarders, and the whole household often socialized together.

Acknowledgements

Much of the inspiration for this collection of writings has come from nature and the scenery surrounding the three communities in which Terry and I have lived and raised our family: Prince Rupert, Terrace, and Castlegar; all in British Columbia. The people of those communities have been, and still are, inspirational. The happy and fulfilling events described in some of these selections reflect the closeness of friends from the neighbourhood, church, work, and our recreational pursuits. Those relationships have helped to generate an atmosphere in which both Terry and I have found a great deal of contentment.

Few people have known that this work was in progress, but my family has always been supportive. My husband Terry has never grumbled at the hours I have spent creating and editing, and has often facilitated things by helping even more than usual. Graham, Jane and Jeremy Fleet have always been encouraging, and Jane and Jeremy have assisted in more specific ways. My brother, Roger Sainsbury, has offered advice and helped in editing. It has been a pleasure working with my illustrator, Sandra Donohue, whose talent, creativity and imagination I have long admired. My thanks to all these individuals, and also to those who have given permission for the publication of certain pieces which mention them by name.

About the Author

Elizabeth Fleet was born in England and educated at Cambridge and Bristol universities. She came to Canada to teach in 1966. She and her husband Terry live in Castlegar, British Columbia. Elizabeth has served on the boards of Selkirk College, the Open Learning Agency/Knowledge Network of British Columbia, and Royal Roads University. In 1996, she was the first Canadian to be awarded the Association of Community College Trustees' Award. Writing, music, cooking and hiking are her favourite spare time pursuits.

About the Illustrator

A former elementary school teacher, Sandra Donohue has always been active in the arts. She began weaving and spinning in the 1970s and began painting seriously in 1997. She is now an Associate member of the Federation of Canadian Artists. Sandra resides in Robson, British Columbia with her husband, Pat.

CPSIA information can be obtained
at www.ICGtesting.com
Printed in the USA
LVHW010905230819
628642LV00003B/3/P